Surfing
and
Spirituality

LESLIE KERBY

Copyright © 2012 Leslie Kerby

All rights reserved.

No part of this report may be reproduced or transmitted in any form whatsoever, electronic, or mechanical, including photocopying, recording, or by any informational storage or retrieval system without express written, dated and signed permission from the author.

Disclaimer and/or Legal Notice: The information presented herein represents the view of the author as of the date of publication. Because of the rate with which conditions change, the author reserves the right to alter and update his opinion based on the new conditions.

The report is for informational purposes only. While every attempt has been made to verify the information provided in this report, neither the author nor her affiliates/partners assume any responsibility for errors, inaccuracies or omissions. Any slights of people or organizations are unintentional. If advice concerning legal, accounting, medical or related matters is needed, the services of a fully qualified professional should be sought. This report is not intended for use as a source of legal, accounting or medical advice. You should be aware of any laws which govern business transactions or other business practices in your country and state.

Note: Names have been changed unless given personal permission to the author.

Kerby, Leslie.
Surfing and Spirituality.

ISBN: 1481075284
ISBN-13: 978-1481075282

Cover Design: © Mitch Bloom

Cover Photos, clockwise from left (front)
1. Mary Osborne; © Justin Bastien
2. Larry Ugale; © David Pu'u
3. Larry Ugale; © David Pu'u
4. Leslie Kerby; © Damon Milazzo
(back) 1. Leslie Kerby; © Kayla Leigh King
2. Ventura Beach; © Leslie Kerby
(inside front title) 1. Mary Osborne; © Justin Bastien
(inside back title) 1. Larry Ugale; © David Pu'u

DEDICATION

This project is dedicated to Michael Rudolph, a friend, mentor and esteemed surfer who went missing in 2006, and whose passion for surfing inspired me to embark on this journey.

CONTENTS

1	My Story	9
2	Introduction	10
3	Culture: So What?	17
4	How I Did It	20
5	The Surfers	23
6	The Verdict	28
7	Nature	30
8	The Spiritual Experience	37
9	The Finale	42
10	Still Hungry?	46

ACKNOWLEDGMENTS

I would like to thank: My family and friends, for encouraging me to follow my own path. Professors Cheleen Mahar and Aaron Greer for their patience, guidance and support. The Elise Eliot Foundation for helping fund my original project. Christian Glasgow, for helping me "Belize" in myself again. Ryan Camana, for unmatched wisdom and guidance. My talented friend Mitch Bloom for an awesome cover. Mary Osborne, Justin Bastien, David Pu'u, Larry Ugale, and Jordan Novander for their supreme generosity with photos. Jaimal Yogis, who participated in interviews and whose book *Saltwater Buddha* inspired me to write my own. And lastly, the fourteen surfers I interviewed, without whom this project would not have been possible. Thank you!

1 MY STORY

Excerpt from *From California to Costa Rica,* Pura Vida:
"*Oh come ON!!!*" I yell, kicking obnoxiously at the unresponsive, salty, dark green mass around me. Blue-lipped, my teeth chattering, I shiver as goose bumps run up my spine, my sun-bleached arm hair standing on end. The deceptive overcast sky mocks me. Though the clouds cover the dusky sun, my sensitive green eyes squint at the bright light the water reflects into my face. Peeking over my left shoulder I see my sister and friends impatiently waiting onshore. *Ignore them. Focus.* I scan the now-empty water. Up ahead, the water swells enough to lift my heart with a glimmer of hope and I inadvertently gasp. "Is it a good one? Please…" I whisper to no one in particular. Anticipating a decent wave, I turn around and start paddling in big, long, hard strokes. Slightly doubting my wave judgment, I glance back at the last second. *No!* In my peripheral vision I catch a glimpse of the face, much too close for comfort. Ditching my board, I dive straight down into the wave right as its lip curls up and over, its breakwater hitting my feet as they go under. The wave tosses and tumbles me like a rag doll, indifferent to the ball of flesh and piece of foam in its path. Feeling the water calm, I kick towards the surface hard, my heart pounding, forcing the last meager air bubbles out of my lungs. No sooner do my lips reach the surface than I gasp noisily for a breath. Waterlogged, frustrated and tired, I scramble for my board (and my senses) and paddle reluctantly for shore, floating in on the punchy whitewash. "That's *it?* What a pathetic session," I mutter to myself, head down, disappointment gnawing at my insides like a ravenous dog on a bone. Indeed, on such days I detest myself, my board and sometimes, most unfairly, even the ocean. Yet without it, and without surfing, I am incomplete, lost. I have personally experienced surfing as it has contributed to shaping my lifestyle, and developing my personality. Infinitely more than simply a sport, hobby or pastime, surfing provides me a means of spirituality.

LESLIE KERBY

2 INTRODUCTION

Don't you realize that the sea is the home of water? All water is off on a journey unless it's in the sea, and it's homesick, and bound to make its way home someday. American folklorist Zora Neale Hurston

I often say I live for the ocean. In Hurston's quote, I am the water; the sea is my home. Separating from the ocean is like separating my soul from my body, my mind from my spirit. Jaimal Yogis' fond recollection of Thomas Farber in his memoir *Saltwater Buddha* conveys this notion well:

'To come back down to the ocean is to reexperience an essential memory trace, something once known well, to recall that one has been trying to remember.' I like that Farber writes 'to recall that *one has been trying to remember'* rather than, *'to recall what one has been trying to remember.' It describes the truth that when away from the sea you can easily forget what you feel homesick for.*

I thoroughly agree. Raised in the coastal community of Ventura, California, I grew up spending every possible second shore-side, in the water. I never tire of the ocean and find supreme difficulty understanding those who do, or those who cannot simply appreciate it in all of its magnificence, grace and glory. My strong relationship with the ocean has manifested itself in many ways, but the one which I am going to discuss here is the sport, art and religion of surfing. Surfing has contributed to shaping my lifestyle and developing my personality, and, most significantly, provides me a means of spirituality.

A common conception in our society is that the spiritual and secular or the sacred and profane realms are oppositional. For example, surfing as a sport is generally considered secular and therefore not spiritual. This study seeks to demonstrate the fallacy of this belief through the observation and analysis of the spiritual capacity of surfing. My goal as an anthropologist is to illustrate how people make spiritual meaning out of surfing. The focus of the study is the connection between surfing as a secular sport and spirituality and asks the question: how is it that surfers find spiritual meaning through their sport and what does this mean with regard to common perceptions of the secular and sacred?

Defining Spirituality

"A strange thing about religion is that we all know what it is until someone asks us to tell them."
– John Bowker, *Oxford Concise Dictionary of World Religions*

Dictionary.com defines spiritual as "of or pertaining to the spirit as the seat of the moral or religious nature," while Encarta defines it as of "the soul or spirit, usually in contrast to material things" and of "religious or sacred things rather than worldly things." Importantly, the last two definitions are stated not in their own light, but in opposition to other ideas. This highlights not only our society's view of the sacred and profane realms as oppositional, but the complexity inherent in defining the concept of spirituality. Rather than being explained, it is defined simply by what it is presumably not, thereby leaving much room for interpretation. German theologian Rudolf Otto concurs with this, stating that "the analogical terminology we use to describe religious experience proves our inability to express it." Religion or the spiritual can be infinitely interpreted; in other words, it is a "collective name," meaning it does not "stand for any single principle or essence." Therefore it would be difficult to define spiritual, religion or the sacred with one abstract definition. Yet, in the words of William James, this "need not prevent me from taking my own narrow view of what religion shall consist in *for the purpose of these lectures*, or, out of the many meanings of the word, from choosing the one meaning in which I wish to interest you particularly, and proclaiming arbitrarily that when I say 'religion' I mean *that*." Hence for our purposes, the spiritual is concerned with personal purpose and meaning. It regards the soul or spirit as the seat of moral or religious nature in a person, that nature being namely concerned with precisely those questions of purpose and meaning. In this study 'spiritual' will therefore also pertain to purpose and meaning, insofar as it is the purpose and meaning one attaches to an object or experience to make it personally meaningful.

With the spiritual defined as concerning meaning in life, spirituality itself in turn refers to any human process which aspires towards enlightenment-- towards answering the all-important question: "What is the meaning of life?" And what is such a question, if not a human one concerning our very existence? In studying spirituality as a human endeavor, we assume that spirituality not only exists but that there is a basic fundamental need for it, a fundamental need to understand ourselves and our place in the universe. We can assume this because life is difficult; we constantly vacillate between good times and bad times. We struggle with what to do with our lives, what career to choose, and which path to take. Unable to rest with the ambiguity of our existence, at some point we have all asked "What's the point [of life]?" This is the inevitable burden of the human condition which all of humanity shares; namely, the fact that we do not inherently know the meaning of our existence. During our life we ask questions like 'Why am I here?' and 'What is my place in the universe?' In other words, 'What is the meaning of life? French psychoanalyst Jacques Lacan calls this desire for enlightenment the *objet petit a*, the unattainable object of desire. Further, professional surfer Rob Machado articulates this well in Taylor Steele's surf film *The Drifter*, saying "we dream of the perfect wave, the perfect job, the perfect house...[but] when we get there, we dream of something else." In other words, whether consciously or subconsciously, through all of the meaningful processes we partake in- our work, our play, our religion- we are searching for ways to transcend this struggle. Yet, as both Lacan and Machado imply, we rarely succeed.

For our purposes we will refer to spirituality as a process of fulfilling this need for understanding of the meaning of existence which is part of the human condition, part of our humanity. As the questioning and answering of one's purpose is a personal process with answers clearly varying from individual to individual, we are concerned with *personal* religion, with the personal spiritual experiences of individual people, in this case surfers'. My purpose in studying surfing is to show how surfers have answered this question for themselves, utilizing their sport as a spiritual process. Therefore the concern here is with demonstrating how surfers contend with ultimate questions of purpose and meaning; in other words, the human condition. My investigation reveals how surfers' desire for spiritual understanding is manifested through their sport.

Spirituality: Modes of Measurement

Yet what exactly does a spiritual process then entail? Although it may not be the only spiritual process, religion undoubtedly is the most commonly accepted form of spirituality, and therefore I find it befitting to consider those spiritual fruits which religion generally bears as the defining factors of what constitute a spiritual process: a quest to know oneself and one's place in the universe. Such spiritual provisions provide us something with which to measure surfing as a proposed form of spirituality. Again, for our purposes spirituality is a process of self-discovery; namely, of the learning and experiencing of *the actor's perception* of life's purpose by the actor.

Religion usually seeks to provide self-discovery through the spiritual experiences of both a transformation of consciousness and a connection to a higher entity. To clarify, by transformation of consciousness, we mean an alteration of mental, physical and/or emotional state; liminality, to cross a threshold. By William James' more broad definition, spiritual experience entails the acts, feelings or experiences of a practitioner in light of *his form of the divine*. Now, as I said earlier, we constantly seek the meaning of life through any number of meaning-making experiences, be it our work, play or religion. Yet rarely do we transcend this struggle of the human condition and reach self-discovery. Rarely do we experience a "transformation of consciousness," something so incredible, transformative and life-changing, that it is ineffable, beyond words. This type of ineffable transcendental experience is what we will consider a spiritual experience, the cornerstone of spirituality. For our purposes then, a spiritual experience involves that which religion usually intends to provide: a transformation of consciousness, usually in the presence of that which one personally considers divine. Spirituality then is a process of self-discovery focusing on the *experience* of the numinous rather than an abstract notion of it.

Importantly, this type of ineffable experience is what differentiates spirituality from other meaning-making processes, and what differentiates surfing from brushing your teeth or from badminton, for example. Surfing is significant through and in the experience. It is ineffable. It is not often one hears of people coming back from brushing their teeth transformed, unable to explain their experience, enlightened. However, all of my informants reportedly have entered into an altered mental physical or emotional state while surfing; that is, experienced a transformation of consciousness, an ineffable experience.

Phenomenology and Symbolism, Myth and Ritual

As it is concerned with the experiential, such an approach to spirituality is often called a phenomenological approach. In the words of anthropologist E.E. Evans-Pritchard, a phenomenological method is "a comparative study of beliefs and rites, such as god, sacrament, and sacrifice, to determine their meaning and social significance." Importantly, my concern is not whether the beliefs and rites of surfers are theologically right or wrong, but what their relational and social import is. In other words, my questions inquire about the society of surfers' beliefs and experiences, rather than their theological truth or falsity.

William James defines religion as "the feelings, acts, and experiences of individual men in their solitude, so far as they apprehend themselves to stand in relation to whatever they may consider the divine." By referring to divinity as relative and conditional to each man's perception he creates a workable definition. In other words, what one man considers divine another may not. The foci of religion for James are, then, person's acts, feelings and experiences in relation to that which he personally considers sacred. As I said before, in this study 'spiritual' pertains to purpose and meaning, insofar as it is the purpose and meaning one attaches to an object or experience to make it personally meaningful or "personally sacred," as James puts it. This relates to my thesis in that surfing, commonly considered secular, of no sacred or divine wealth, is indeed considered divine, spiritual or religious by many surfers; for them it is personally meaningful and transcendental experientially.

Therefore more than discovering the myths, symbols and rituals in surfing, we are interested in why they exist, what import they hold. We are concerned with what meaning they carry for actors within their culture. For example, concerning the "dawn patrol" surfing ritual, one might inquire as to why a surfer awakens at dawn daily to greet the waves.[1] Is it because he or she likes to wake up early? Or is it out of respect for his or her spiritual provider, the ocean? Or is it for another reason?

Yet again I want to emphasize the fact that religion and spirituality are, in a sense, indefinable, and as William James so perfectly states,

we are dealing with a field of experience where there is not a single conception that can be sharply drawn....things are more or less divine, states of mind are more or less religious, reactions are more or less total, and it is everywhere a question of amount and degree. Nevertheless...the divinity of the object and solemnity of the reaction or too well marked for doubt. Hesitation as to whether a state of mind is 'religious,' or 'irreligious,' or 'moral,' or 'philosophical,' is only likely to arise when the state of mind is weakly characterized, but in that case it will be hardly worthy of our study at all.

In other words, though we cannot clearly define the spiritual, we *can* delineate our interpretation and, studying potentially spiritual experiences, determine their spiritual capacity or essence against our delineated realm of reason. While I could not argue as James does that the divinity of an experience or object is always recognizable, I do take my conclusions from my informants who judge their own experiences as spiritual or not, and their surfing as spiritual or not.

Additionally I compare the surfing experience with other religions and philosophies, insofar as my informants do so themselves. This includes drawing parallels between surfing and religions like Buddhism, in order to demonstrate the veracity of spiritual provisions prevalent in surfing.

---

[1] "Dawn patrol- to be on the beach or in the water at sunrise. Usually used as a tactical maneuver to beat the crowds. Many surfers also value the quiet, contemplative beauty of surfing at daybreak." From Matt Warshaw's *The Encyclopedia of Surfing*. (150)

The Secular vs. Sacred: Sport

Sport, or the secular as sacred, is a relatively radical idea in our society today. We favor designating people, things and ideas to categories. On the one hand this is imperative for us as humans so that each day or even each experience is not chaotic. Thus, we differentiate among things by drawing information and then categorizing. The problem is that we tend to accept these labels as final, sometimes inflexibly boxing people and concepts into set positions, and hindering their mobility. For example, secular has been defined as "without spiritual or religious capacity" and sport is commonly categorized as secular. According to this definition the secular cannot then produce the spiritual. No one wants to see sport transcending the boundaries of secularism. It would defy established definitions and complicate the mass cultural ideology, making things difficult to understand. As one surfer, Aaron, succinctly put it, "If people can find liberation through sport, why go to church?" "Everything has its place" is the standard, if outdated, ideal. Personally I think this mentality hinders one from encountering potentially spiritual experiences in everyday life through "secular" activities such as surfing. Through the acts, feelings and experiences which we commit ourselves to as they are personally meaningful for us, be it our work, our religion, our circle of friends and family, our sport or play, we are often times in fact creating for ourselves, whether consciously or subconsciously, a sort of spirituality. We are searching and finding meaning in our lives through and in certain experiences in order to alleviate the yoke of the human condition.

Sport as Sacred: Surfing

Obviously, posing the concept that surfing is a means of spirituality goes against not only dictionary definitions but societal rules. Traditionally, people have turned to religion to answer questions concerning spirituality. Probably due to the way our society has defined secular and spiritual, the common belief is that the spiritual is religious—and therefore not within a secular process. Nonetheless an ever-growing subset of surfers within the larger global surfing community considers surfing to be more of a spiritual experience than a simple leisure activity, more of a religion than a sport. Many such surfers would agree that simply calling surfing a sport marginalizes it, undermining its powerful spiritual capacity. I ask, why? Why is it that we as a society do not associate religion with sport, the secular with the sacred? In reality, religion is just *one* possible way in which people experience spirituality. Surfing is another.

For example, Professor-surfer Bron Taylor argues in his article *Surfing into Spirituality and a New, Aquatic Nature Religion* that the "physical, psychological, and spiritual" benefits of surfing are so profound that surfing "should be understood as a new religious movement" which he calls "Aquatic Nature Religion." Significant parallels have also been drawn between surfing and Asian religions such as Buddhism. Professor-surfer Peter Kreeft argues that surfing makes one mystical, likening the "stoke or high of surfing to the concept of Nirvana or enlightenment in Buddhism." My research investigates the many ways people use surfing as spirituality. Accordingly I suggest that although surfing is commonly perceived as a secular activity, its multifaceted ritualistic culture renders it a promising spiritual process. Moreover, I hypothesize that surfing, as a spiritual experience, provides one path to answering the burden of the human condition as well as demonstrates the secular as sacred.

When I speak of surfing as a multifaceted, ritualistic culture, I mean that it is a complex set of symbols, myths and rituals deeply meaningful for members. Here I borrow from the field of symbolic and interpretive anthropology a viewpoint of culture as a system of symbols reflecting values, and human behavior as symbolic action. In this case the human behavior is then surfing. An analysis of culture is seen as, in the words of Clifford Geertz, "an interpretive one, in search of meaning". The goal is to understand culture as do one's informants, in order to begin to understand local meaning. By taking an interpretive-symbolic approach to the symbols, myths and rituals in surfing, I intend to unpack the complex cultural package of surfing to glean the local, or emic, meaning.

Topics of Concern-Negative Aspects of Surfing

Before discussing the results of my research it is important to note that that there are indeed other facets to the surfing culture, many of which display far from spiritual qualities. Problems such as over-competitiveness, localism and fighting, even to the extent of "surf terrorism," as surfer George put it, are significant issues in surfing. However, though in need of addressing, they are not the foci of this investigation, and therefore will not be discussed.

3 CULTURE: SO WHAT?

Culture inevitably shapes those who act within it. In the words of Max Weber, "Man is an animal suspended in webs of significance which he himself has spun," meaning that one creates meaning out of one's own behavior; we are trapped by our own thoughts, actions, and words. The knowledge, values, beliefs and attitudes of a culture are often reflected in the ritual behavior which the actors of that culture partake in; in other words, rituals reflect values. Like any other culture, surfing is a complex myriad of symbols, rituals and myths deeply significant for participants and believers. Superficially, out of context, these signs or rituals, such as paddling out into the ocean or riding a wave, do not carry much meaning. It is only once they are viewed within the context of their own culture or subculture[2] that they become meaningful. In order to glean the local meaning from a culture like surfing, one must first observe, experience and understand the culture as the participants themselves do. Then, by analyzing the ritual behavior of the actors in a culture, we can begin to understand the purpose of this behavior for the actors themselves.

This method of analyzing culture is labeled as an interpretive and symbolic anthropological approach. Especially helpful corresponding works have been written by Clifford Geertz and Victor Witter Turner, both pioneers in this method of cultural anthropology.

An Interpretive Approach to Culture

Clifford Geertz establishes a general interpretive and symbolic approach to culture in his book entitled *The Interpretation of Cultures: Selected Essays* (1973). For Geertz, culture manifests as a scheme of symbols and meanings visibly portrayed in both objects and actions. Geertz sees human behavior as symbolic action, "action which…signifies" and states that in observing symbolic actions one should ask "what their import is: what it is, ridicule or challenge, irony or anger, snobbery or pride, that, in their occurrence and through their agency, is getting said." In other words, how does symbolic action reveal the thoughts and attitudes of the actor? How does this, in turn, reflect the thoughts and attitudes of the culture in which the actor is a member? The goal, according to Geertz, is to understand culture within the same circumstance as the subjects in order to become knowledgeable of the local meanings. He proposes that in order for us to understand how people think, act and live, we must get as close to those people as possible.

The essential vocation of interpretive anthropology is not to answer our deepest questions, but to make available to us answers that others, guarding other sheep in other valleys, have given, and thus to include them in the consultable record of what man has said.

In other words, our anthropological purpose in symbolically interpreting culture is not to answer life's greatest mysteries but to study, comprehend and depict the way certain cultures have answered such questions for themselves. Correspondingly this applies to this study of surfing in that this study intends not to answer the question "what is the meaning of life" but to show how surfers have approached this question for themselves through their own symbolic, ritualistic culture. In the words of Henry David Thoreau quoted by Geertz, "It is not worth it to go round the world to count the cats in Zanzibar." In other words, what is the point of observation without questioning the significance or meaning of that which one observes?

This is a question inherent to cultural anthropology and to this study. Cultural analysis for Geertz is "not an experimental science in search of law but an interpretive one in search of meaning." One should question not only what a human behavior is, but its significance for those whom experience it. For example, in relation to human behavior, one should ask: what is the meaning of this action within its context? What does this mean for the actor? A question one might ask in the research of spirituality in surfing, then, is not: what is surfing? but rather: what does surfing mean?

Symbolism and Ritual

Victor Witter Turner argues more specifically the importance of symbolism and ritual in cultural analysis in a fashion akin to Geertz in his work *Blazing the Trail: Way Marks in The Exploration of Symbols* (1992). He discusses the significance of ritual in detail, stating such important traits as the meaning of ritual to natives within their culture, its transformative capacity, its spontaneity, its responsiveness to present circumstance and its competence to interpret current situations and provide viable ways of coping with contemporary problems. Turner also showcases the various ways in which symbolism can explain a culture, explicate its ethos, and reflect its values. For example, according to Turner, verbal and nonverbal language such as sight, smell, touch, taste and kinetic experience as well as hearing, are all human behaviors "exploited for their symbolic wealth" and we "human beings exploit the total sensorium for our communicative codes." From this view any and every aspect of human behavior contains some significance.

His methodology involves ethnography and on-site field work in Africa and other regions around the world. One of his main conclusions in the study of cultures is that

> ...*human beings are relational creatures and cannot be validly studied apart from the network of love and interest in which they are incessantly involved.*

This statement reflects how Turner, like Geertz, believes that in order to comprehend the actions, feelings and ideas of a culture's people, one must consider both the people and their behavior within the context of that corresponding culture. A person's idiosyncrasies cannot be comprehended when separated from his or her unique background.

Turner suggests that in certain cases, existing theoretical apparatuses such as Durkheimian, for instance, lack the depth necessary in analyzing symbols and rituals. Influenced by psychoanalyst and religion critic Sigmund Freud, Turner also applies the interpretive approach to religion. For example, in relation to the notion of a "'religion of psychoanalysis'" previously proposed by various psychoanalysts in the field, Turner asks: why can't psychoanalysis be a religion? And, what constitutes religion? -- questions which correlate with the prospect of the secular (here psychoanalysis) associating with the sacred (here religion). I am proposing a similar prospect here, suggesting surfing (the secular) as spiritual or sacred.

4 HOW I DID IT

"It is not worth it to go round the world to count the cats in Zanzibar." – Henry David Thoreau

    As Thoreau so aptly noted and as far as my research is concerned, in the search for the meaning of and reasoning behind human behavior, one may find great difficulty when only provided with thinly described people, places and things. In other words, the potential is limited in answering the question of what an action signifies, what its import is, when only the date, time and place are given. In the words of Clifford Geertz, "Cultural analysis is guessing at meanings, assessing the guesses, and drawing explanatory conclusions from the better guesses, not discovering the Continent of Meaning and mapping out its bodiless landscape." In qualitative research, the purpose lies with the *why* and *how* of things rather than merely the *what, where* and *when*. Therefore the concern is not only with what something (or someone) looks like, its instance and its location, but what it means in the cultural context of its existence. We care not so much that an elephant is large and gray but that it means a memorable zoo animal to one person and a holy venerated god to another.

    Because I am not only interested in what surfing is but why people surf and how they make meaning out of surfing, especially spiritually, the interpretive methodology is appropriate. Moreover, for my purposes the methods to gain insight into the connection between surfing and spirituality are inductive, ethnographically based methods and involve both literary research as well as fieldwork, with the emphasis on the latter. My main focus, both in the literary and everyday sense, is on surfers' personal narratives. My fieldwork consists namely of participant observation, open-ended and structured interviews. I participated in and observed surfing. Though some interviews felt like normal conversations, while others were more formal, I used the same set questions in each. Nothing more than a pencil, paper, and sometimes a tape recorder, when we met face to face, was used during these interviews. I say "when we met face to face" because some interviews were done by email or telephone rather than in person.

Because I have already experienced the surf culture, I located informants first by contacting surfers whom I already knew and then, following the methodology of snowball sampling, I obtained more contacts. Snowball sampling is appropriate here as a nonprobability sampling technique and is commonly used in qualitative field research when members of a special population are difficult to locate. Therefore I first informally contacted acquaintances and while it was possible that they would suggest to me further contacts, this was neither expected nor obligatory. These ethnographic methods allowed themes and topics to emerge from the data themselves, helping me in understanding the actors' background, attitudes and actions, and consequently their local significance.

I analyzed my data while also collecting data, interpreting and reporting. Hence I simultaneously collected both textual and live information from the field, sorted through it, format it into a larger picture, interpreted it and wrote my qualitative analysis. For me "textual" refers to all literary works as well as film, and "live" refers to interviews, both by email, telephone or in-person. I sorted the volume of data including interview transcriptions, observational notes, documents and visual material, into themes and patterns to categorize and then interpret, working from large to small, to large again, to emerge with a meaningful picture.

Because we are all thinking beings, our experiences and perspectives inevitably shape our data; thus in explaining my methodology I feel it is important to note my position in relation to surfing and spirituality. I personally have experienced surf culture as it has greatly affected my lifestyle, especially spiritually. This is an ongoing process and my life-long relationship with the ocean has provided and continues to provide me with a sense of well-being, purpose and significance incomparable to any other culture or activity. The meaningful weight which surf culture bears on my life (and my fascination with it), is namely what inspired me to research surfing as a spiritual form, my personal example of the secular as sacred. I was keen to know whether and how others have experienced the surf culture in a spiritual manner and what this means in relation to the larger discussion of what defines spirituality and how it can or cannot be experienced.

In fact, already there have been significant contributions made to the discussion of surfing and spirituality and my preliminary conclusions about surfing as an example of the secular as sacred are replicated in existing literature. Because the size of my study is relatively small, no sweeping generalizations will be made. Yet however limited my data might be, the replication of such a project is possible and I hope that my research on this topic will inspire others in the field of anthropology to conduct similar studies. Potential projects might investigate the relationship between the secular and sacred within the larger realm of spirituality, or the topic of surfing specifically as an example of spirituality and the secular as sacred.

5 THE SURFERS

From September through February 2009 I formally interviewed fourteen participants from all walks of life, from different locations all over the world, with an age range spanning half a century. They all have one thing common: they surf. I interviewed these men and women with the intention of investigating the relationship between surfing and spirituality. I wanted to know whether, how and why surfers make spiritual meaning out of surfing. The interviews ranged temporally from 30 to 90 minutes and from one to eight pages in length. I used the same set of questions for each interview, the first four of which were more general and open-ended, the second seven of which were more structured.[3] I interviewed seven people in person, four by email and three by telephone. These interviews, as primary sources, provide the bulk of my evidence, in the art of spoken word as text. Therefore, just as one writes a literature review to familiarize the reader with literary works one intends to reference, I would like to briefly introduce you, the reader, to my informants. I found their generosity in sharing with me their first-hand experience invaluable.

Respondent Profiles

I found Chad's email address on the editor's page of my SURFING magazine. A 32-year old native Californian transplanted to Indonesia via surfing, he is a writer/journalist and SURFING Magazine's "Bali Guy." His life "pretty much revolves around surfing" and he considers surfing very spiritual, especially in the sense of building a relationship with nature. He stands firmly behind the mantra "NATURE = GOD," adding that "If surfing's not religious, then I'm not religious."

Chad referred me to another SURFING magazine editor, Michael. A 38-year old California-born surfer who grew up in Virginia Beach, he spoke with me on the phone. Now living in North Carolina, he has surfed for 30 years and written for surfing magazines the past 15 of those 30. His favorite part of surfing is the "escape." He refers to surfing as "a celebratory

---

[3] See Appendix A for interview questions.

pursuit- whether in celebration of that moment, that day or that wave."

I picked up Steve's book when I began this project and proceeded to contact him via his website; we spoke on the phone. He is a 42-year old East Coast native now in New Mexico. He is a writer, surfer and science guru whose experience surfing helped him battle Lyme disease. His fascination with the sport led him on a three-year quest around the world into the science and spirituality of surfing. Though scientifically he says sports such as downhill mountain biking spark "flow-states" or chemical highs similar to surfing, there is still an inexplicable "noetic inch"[4] or higher element to surfing that makes it unique.

In my interview with Steve, he referred me to Dan, a surfer from a large surfing family based out of Sydney, Australia. A 45-year old surfer-intellectual, he has surfed all his life. Dan established a complex surfing philosophy called "surfism" that "views existence in terms corresponding to surfing." He talks about the art of surfboard design, the ritual feeling in putting on a wetsuit and "waxing up" [your surfboard], and the warrior mentality necessary in big waves: "it feels like you're preparing for battle, your wetsuit like your suit of armor, your board a shield." He finds camaraderie in surfing but sees it as insignificant in comparison to the act of surfing itself. He also notes the excitement in talking about weather and anticipating waves pre-surf.

Jaimal, 30, grew up in Portugal and California until he ran away from home to Hawaii at age 16 on a quest for both spirituality and surfing. He is a Zen Buddhist-surfer-journalist living in San Francisco. I picked up his book this summer while browsing through the surfing section at my local Barnes and Noble. It inspired me and I contacted him initially through e-mail and thereafter by telephone. For him, surfing "takes priority over almost everything." He sees it as a symbol of freedom, and says it helps him grow spiritually because it "gives you this feeling of being part of something larger." He compares surfing to a meditation because one is focused on nothing else, one is "hyper-present." He also notes how interacting with the ocean is different from a cliff or mountain, something stationary: "the ocean is rocking you as much as you are rocking it."

My neighbor Tory, 43, grew up in Ventura, California, and has been surfing for 35 years. He is a teacher-surf instructor and environmentalist. We chatted over breakfast burritos and coffee (classic surfer grub) at a surf spot in Ventura. For him, surfing is very spiritual: "believing that we

---

[4] Steve refers to "noetic inch" here as the existential component of the surfing experience (often referred to as "the feeling" or "stoke" in surfing) thus far unexplained by science. For more on Noetic Theory or Noëtics see the Institute of Noetic Sciences website at http://www.noetic.org/about/what_is.cfm.

crawled out of the ocean thousands of years ago, it's nice to crawl back in once or twice a day." His personal surfing mentality is to "respect people and the environment and to stay humble." He has an appreciation for all types of surfing and takes pleasure in "sharing the stoke" of surfing with others- in other words, teaching others to surf, bringing others into the water, often in hopes that they will learn to appreciate and respect the "Mother" ocean as well.

Aaron, 38, was a personal acquaintance whom I interviewed in person at a café. He grew up and learned to surf in Northern California and now surfs in Oregon. He is a professor and has been surfing for 20 years. For him surfing is "so distinct from skating and snowboarding" because of the feeling of anticipation when waiting for waves. That feeling is something found only in surfing. For him surfing is about surrendering to the wave rather than fighting or trying to conquer it. He tries to be giving in the water but struggles with becoming too aggressive; however, he sees this as a positive result of surfing because it has forced him to assess negative character traits of his personality. He finds surfing to be very spiritual, but does not like the use of the term "religion" when describing surfing.

I interviewed my neighbor Kristi, 30, in her front yard. Surfing the past 11 years, she works for the environmental surfing organization Surfrider Foundation. She has a lot of respect for the Hawaiian surf culture and tries to uphold the "aloha spirit." Surfing for her is to "play," to have a "peaceful experience...connect with nature." She describes surfing as "satisfying, almost like an addiction...there's definitely something that's satisfied when you surf and you feel fulfilled in a way that you didn't before you went surfing." She likes the noncompetitive nature of surfing.

Dick, 50, is a Venice, California, native with an extensive background in almost every corner of surfing over the past 42 years. He has surfed competitively and professionally, worked as editor of SURFER magazine and continues to write and publish surf-related work to this day. Because he wrote the only legitimate encyclopedia of surfing I have found, I contacted him through his website, by e-mail. At this point he thinks "people freight the sport with more than it really should bear," noting that "[he] certainly did - - for 20-30 years." Surfing's purpose for him has changed over the years from a "social thing, to a competitive outlet, to an excuse to travel, to an identity." "More than that," he says, "and always, from the beginning, I just love being in a wave zone; changing environments, from land to water. And I love doing something where I've at least got a chance at a graceful moment or two." He does not find surfing more spiritual than other nature-based activities.

I have greatly admired 28-year-old professional surfer Mary since high school. Also a Ventura native, I contacted her through e-mail and interviewed her in her home office. She finds surfing "extremely emotional" and "definitely spiritual." She attributes some character traits such as respect, open-mindedness, and a sense of gratitude to surfing. She talks about a lot of the disunity in surfing currently and how it's important to remember that "we're all out there for the same reason- to have fun, be in nature."

I heard about and contacted George, 59, through e-mail before interviewing him in his home office. A teacher by profession, he has been surfing for 45 years in Santa Monica and Oxnard and co-founded two nonprofit surfing organizations- the Surfrider Foundation and the Groundswell Society. He is opposed to the turning of surfing into a religion and also to the use of surfing to make money. "And that's because waves are for free. Anybody who's trying to extract something from the ocean is taking something and using it for their own benefit, even though it was free and they didn't own it, and even though they didn't do anything to make it better for anybody else." He finds the most important thing in life and in surfing is to do something for the good of humankind. He says "There's unity [in surfers] and yet there's complete disunity. The only basic connection is that everybody needs the ocean." Surfing is completely interwoven to what he does and he finds there are both positive and negative traits he has learned from it, all paradoxical: humility, patience, health, given incredible amount of energy, and yet also arrogance, flippant sarcasm, ego-inflation and "a general sense of superiority to people who don't surf."

I went to high school with Mitch, 21, and interviewed him at a café in Ventura as well as on the phone. He has been surfing for 10 years, works in surf shops and surfs on a daily basis. He compares surfing to a meditation, "in the fact that it's probably one of the only things in the world that you can do where you're not thinking about anything else in the world but that." Surfing for him is fun and relaxing. The main reason he loves it as compared to other sports is "It's not competitive! Surfing itself is not competitive until you throw a contest in the mix...99% of the surfing population isn't competitive." He sees it as kind of a selfish sport: "the purpose is self-fulfillment, the main reason you're driving to the beach every day is for yourself, no one else."

My neighbor Bob, 55, is from Burbank but grew up surfing in Santa Monica as well as hitchhiking to Malibu in the late 1960s and early 1970s to surf. He now surfs Ventura whenever he can. I interviewed him at his home. For him surfing is a lifestyle. He recognizes that it is spiritual for some people, but for him it just means great fun. His surfing mentality is positive and he takes the motto "the best surfer in the water is the one having the most fun" to heart.

I interviewed my neighbor Richard, 64, through e-mail. A teacher by profession, surfing has been a constant in his life for 52 years. Part of surfing's first growth surge on the West coast, he says surfing can be a "'Religion' to some, not in the sense of looking for a 'god' for providing; rather finding that the nature (god's creation) of riding a wave can be unbelievably fulfilling. The 'fulfillment' is not just physical; it's mental, emotional and psychological as well." He appreciated the "fraternity" among surfers back in the 1960s and longs for the day when one could still find "uncrowded waves."

The range of variation between the fourteen surfers' perceptions of surfing in their lives ranged from a just-for-fun, lifestyle-based perception to a very religious or spiritual perception. On a spectrum between extreme competitiveness with no spiritual connection whatsoever and extreme spirituality or religiosity, no surfers landed at either extreme. The surfers fell into three groups; those perceiving surfing as a fun lifestyle, those perceiving it as a spiritual lifestyle and those who considered their surfing to be very spiritual. Three surfers, Bob, Richard and Dick, fell into the first category. Five surfers, Mitch, Mary, Dan, George and Kristi, fell into the second. Six surfers, Jaimal, Aaron, Steve, Tory, Michael and Chad fell into the third. No surfers refuted the claim that surfing is spiritual in some sense. Also, the vast majority of surfers, twelve out of fourteen, found it personally spiritual in some way and mentioned experiencing a spiritual experience while surfing at least once before.

6 THE VERDICT

Surfing is really more than anything else a faith. –*SURFER* editor Sam George

  I initially entered into this project and my interviews with the hope that I could understand the phenomenon of surfing better. Questions I posed included 'Why do people devote themselves to surfing so religiously? What does it mean to surf? Why does it matter?' I suspected from personal experience and initial research, that surfing had aspects which could lead it to be considered spiritual despite its standard connotation as secular. When viewed through an interpretive symbolic anthropological lens,[5] surfing could be analyzed as a complex symbolic, ritualistic cultural system, the center of which I predicted spirituality[6] lay. Significantly, this suspicion went against established social and cultural ideologies which by definition oppose the secular and the spiritual.[7] This then also posed the question 'what is spirituality? What qualifies as sacred?' Through my research using first-hand participant observation, literature and interviews, I investigated further and have developed hypothetical answers to my questions.
  I redefined spirituality as any process aspiring towards enlightenment, centered around and culminating in the ineffable transcendental experience. This experience involves in particular the spiritual provisions of a connection with that which one considers divine, transformation of consciousness, and self discovery. Surfing, as an ineffable experience,

---

[5] An interpretive symbolic lens views culture as a system of symbols reflecting values, and human behavior as symbolic action. See page 11 of Introduction and Geertz, *An Interpretation of Cultures,* page 5.

[6] Spirituality, as defined on page 6 in the introduction, refers to any human process which aspires towards enlightenment.

[7] See pages 5-10 of the Introduction for more on the secular versus sacred opposition.

qualifies. Again, the purpose in this investigation is to refute the common belief that the secular cannot be sacred by showing surfing as an example of the secular as sacred, and thereby present, most importantly, an opportunity to look at spirituality in a different light than we are commonly accustomed to in western society, an opportunity to redefine spirituality.

7 NATURE

NATURE=GOD – Tom Blake, pioneer surfer

That spiritual experiences are not only possible, but likely in surfing, becomes more apparent when one considers the environment in which surfing takes place. It becomes yet more apparent when considering the fact that the possibility of surfing occurring at all depends entirely upon the very specific conditions of that constantly changing environment at a very specific moment in time. In surfing, the *environment* in which the act of surfing takes place is as important as the act of surfing itself.

The ocean creates for many surfers a realm of opportunity for transcendental experiences and ultimately enlightenment. In this section I will focus mainly on surfers' experiences connecting with their form of the divine, the ocean, and the ways the ocean creates an environment in which transcendental experiences occur. Recurring themes which surfers expressed in my interviews included feelings of awe, respect, gratitude and love for the ocean. In the surfing realm of belief, the ocean can mean something sacred, revered, feared, respected, appreciated or loved. Surfers also reported a sense of humility and personal empowerment developing out of their oceanic experiences, the former from surrendering to, and the latter from surviving and harnessing, the waves.

Awe: Raw Power and Ancient Wisdom
Nothing in the world is more flexible and yielding than water. Yet when it attacks the firm and the strong, none can withstand it. They have no way to change it. - The Tao Te Ching

The ocean is, among other things, a massive, salty, moving body of water covering most of earth. It can be the scariest or the most beautiful thing. No one can deny the power, strength and force the ocean holds, nor the history, knowledge and potential wisdom. As surfer George urges, Go out into the ocean and squint your eyes and kind of look at it...you can see something that's been there for 20,000 years! There is indeed a timeless reality to waves-they're living fossils! It's the past right in front of you!" In other words, the ocean is a real, tangibly available, completely free entity which is also ancient, as old as time as we know it. More importantly, as such, it offers immeasurable opportunities for learning, growth, and powerful experiences. From a surfer's perspective, the ocean is alive. It can be calm, peaceful, soothing, but also a powerful, forceful source of energy.

Through surfing, George continues, one "gets to be in direct contact with energy systems which are literally the largest sources of power on the planet, so it's special on an objective scale because it represents an extraordinary opportunity for a human being that really can't be accessed in other ways." In other words, because the ocean contains immeasurable power incomparable to other "sources of power on the planet," directly connecting with it as surfers do is an utterly unique, rare opportunity. Note that he uses the term "opportunity," suggesting that connecting with the ocean creates a state of possibility, a chance for prospective events to occur.

More than experientially rare for a human being, Jaimal feels that the energy experienced while surfing stays with him after he gets out of the water. Like George, he notes the ocean as a major source of energy:

I think we receive this energy from the waves, like we take some of their momentum, like we're tapping into this major energy source when riding. Even if you have a bad day surfing, it's still good when you get out. That surf, saltwater high- you take some of the ocean energy with you.

In surfing one not only connects to this powerful energy source, but absorbs some of its energy. Surfers like Jaimal attribute these post-surf feelings of energy to the ocean's power, recognizing, appreciating and even venerating the ocean in gratitude. Even on bad days surfers enjoy their feat. Like Jaimal says, "Even if you have a bad day surfing"-meaning even on days when one catches no waves, merely survives them- the ocean still shares its energy, makes one feel good, enticing one to return for more. Just surviving the ocean can spark gratitude.

Nonetheless, as George notes, while inspiring appreciation, surviving also provides an ego-boost, spurring self-confidence. This is because surviving the ocean is an obstacle in itself.

[Surfing is] a great way to live philosophically...the surfer's mentality- you just don't take no for an answer. When you think of the fundamental act of surfing, when you paddle out into the ocean, the ocean tells you 'No, go back to the beach! No, go back to the beach! No, don't come out here! No, this isn't where you're supposed to be!' Realistically, you've got to have a lot of faith in yourself, [be] really self-confident [to surf].

In other words, surfing is fundamentally a process of overcoming constant difficulty, in the form of incessantly rushing waves. The surf zone ranges from annoyingly difficult to terrifying, but in any case facing and overcoming these waves can breed confidence. It can instill a strong-minded mentality which "doesn't take no for an answer," one applicable to all facets of life.

Fear: Feeling Small, Surrender and Humility

Jack London brings the humbling experience of facing the ocean to life in his famed essay *A Royal Sport*, describing his first encounter with surfing in Hawaii,

Indeed, one feels microscopically small, and the thought that one may wrestle with this sea raises in one's imagination a thrill of apprehension, almost fear. Why they are a mile long, these bull-mouthed monsters, and they weigh a thousand tons, and they charge into shore faster than a man can run. What chance? No chance at all, is the verdict of the shrinking ego.

In other words the prospect of facing the ocean brings forth strong feelings of personal insignificance, anxiety and even fear. The ocean can be a daunting environment, even for the most experienced surfer. As professional surfer Rob Machado relates in the film *The Drifter* by Taylor Steele, "One day I decided to paddle alone between these two islands…and halfway across I found myself too tired to continue. I stopped paddling and just sat there. I'd never felt so insignificant in my whole life."

Rudolf Otto describes religious experience as presenting "itself as something wholly other; nothing human or cosmic. Man feels a profound nothingness." In other words, a religious or spiritual experience distinguishes itself by appearing as something completely novel, ineffable, and by inducing in one a feeling of intense insignificance or nonexistence, by making one feel "small," per se. Otto's type of religious experience, the feeling of a "profound nothingness" in the presence of something "other," can be likened to those of Rob Machado and Jack London, the feeling of insignificance a surfer feels floating about in the enormous ocean, paddling through walls of water, often tossing like a ragdoll in a washing machine. One is at the whim of the ocean; one's life in nature's hands. Hence, according to Otto, we here see an example of surfing as a religious experience, as well as an example of the secular as sacred.

The ocean's intimidation often results positively in the development of humility as well as a respect for the ocean, in the surfer. As Tory contends about Hawaiian waves, some of the largest, strongest and most threatening in the world, "I'm really humbled by the power of the waves over there." Also, when asked how he had personally grown from surfing, Tory confirmed "the biggie is humility." Many surfers experience humility the same way people experience humility religiously. It could be said that where others have God, surfers have the Ocean. Tory continued, saying that by relinquishing control and surrendering to the ocean, "It makes you feel small, not so big-headed and overly important in this world, because of the power of the sea." Surfers know that what the ocean gives- a breath of life, immeasurable energy and strength- the ocean can also take away. Mother Nature is precious and powerful. As Aaron warns, only half-jokingly, "If you curse at the ocean, you had better apologize louder!"

Surfing and Surviving: Personal Empowerment

Let Go or Be Dragged – American Proverb

<u>*Feeling like Part of Something Larger*</u>

Yet the surfing experience becomes a sought-after challenge, novelty, fear and surrender included. As George related earlier, surviving such difficulty breeds confidence. Further, to not only survive but then surf waves, to "move through space effortlessly by virtue of harnessing a natural source of power," as he describes it, not only breeds confidence but makes surfers feel like they are part of something larger. It makes them feel like a part of this energy force they harness, a part of the ocean. Jaimal agrees that surfing "gives you this feeling of being a part of something larger, of being a part of 'God,' or whatever." While humbled by waves' strength and power, surfers feel special and privileged because they get to share that power, the power of a "force bigger than you," as Jaimal says.

Likewise, when asked whether he thought surfing was spiritual, Aaron reasoned that "It's very spiritual, just me and the ocean, a connection with something bigger than me. I recognize that it [the ocean] is more powerful and it's living, and I surrender to it and do not try to control or contain it." Through exposure and interaction with the power and strength of the ocean, surfers learn respect while strengthening and empowering themselves.

<u>*Art: Dancing with the Sea*</u>

Surfer-writer Steve declares surfing a privilege, stating "The Ocean is this big, ferocious, awesome power, and you get to dance with that. Sitting in the water at sunset with glass-off…I know of no better experience."[8]

---

[8] "Glass-off- when the wind calms and the water becomes smooth and glassy." From Matt Warshaw, *The Encyclopedia of Surfing*.

Note how he anthropomorphizes the ocean, using the word "dance," as though the ocean is alive. Tory does much the same, saying "I can ride a longboard however I want, let the wave be the judge, the work is taken away from me." It is as though the wave has a mind of its own, "judging" his surfing and doing the "work." In other words, there is only so much power a surfer has in surfing a wave before the ocean takes over. It's a balancing act between surfer and wave, but the wave has the reigns.

In fact, many surfers describe surfing as beautiful, graceful, a dance with the sea. Jaimal describes it as "masculine and a physical challenge, but also a dance, can be beautiful, an art form, progressive." Surf writer Dick concurs, "I love doing something where I've at least got a chance at a graceful moment or two." The ocean provides the opportunity to turn oneself into a piece of art, to create art together with the ocean, to perform the proverbial miracle of *walking on water*. Quoted in *The Encyclopedia of Surfing*, surfer and board-shaper Dave Parmenter declared in 1998 "There are only two authentically American art forms- jazz and longboarding." [9] Additionally, professional surfer Mary observes her reasoning for longboarding as "I liked the way longboarding felt, that it looked really feminine…it's elegant, it was pretty, pleasing on the eye." Surfers appreciate the opportunity not only to connect with a greater power, but to create something beautiful and graceful in conjunction with that power, be it art or a dance.

Water World: Changing Environments

The way surfers act and react constantly with the ocean's moving surface, this "really pure interface," as Steve puts it, makes it an intricate balancing of give-and-take, a sort of relationship, a "dance" between the surfer and the sea. Interacting with and reacting to a constantly moving surface, as one does in surfing, puts the sport on a different level of difficulty comparatively from other sports and in a different realm generally from other land-based experiences and perspectives. When asked why he surfs, Dick responds, "I just love being in a wave zone, changing environments from land to water." The focus is on the ocean environment, the significance in the difference between land- and water-based perspectives. As Jaimal declares, "The ocean is a unique environment- it's not like a cliff with mountain climbing or a mountain with snowboarding, which is stationary- the ocean is rocking you as much as you're rocking it."

---

[9] "Longboarding- type of surfing performed on a blunt-nosed surfboard, generally over nine feet long…patterned after the style-conscious form of waveriding popular in the early and mid-1960s." From Warshaw.

Steve elaborates, "You commit to an altered reality, almost, with its own different rules, co-created with the ocean. You give up to the source." When stepping into the water, surfers enter a different world, one commanded by the ocean. As he says, "You give up to the source," meaning one surrenders to the ocean, a source of strength and power but also beauty and grace. Yet in surfing it, one intimately interacts with that source, creating a sort of temporary mini-world, a world "co-created with the ocean". Hence surfers, as we have discovered, feel small, succumb and surrender to the ocean, developing humility and respect for it. However, they simultaneously partake in a unique interaction with the sea, one which often leads them to feel special, privileged and empowered. In harnessing the power of the ocean to surf, surfers themselves feel like part of that big, meaningful power source too.

Reverence, Gratitude and Love: Mother Ocean

Mother I never knew
Every time I see the ocean
Every time
-Bosho, 17th Century Zen monk and poet

Many surfers venerate the ocean, personifying it as *Mother Ocean*, even regarding it as a deity figure. Surfing is their connection with the divine. Respect, love and appreciation are key elements of their relationship with the sea. Chad affirms, "In the end, it all comes down to what [surfer] Tom Blake carved into a stone in the mid-west somewhere back in 1920-something: 'NATURE = GOD'."[10] Chad and Tom render nature, and more specifically the ocean, divinity. Surf instructor Tory explains about his relationship with the ocean, "From my personal belief that we crawled out of the ocean millions of years ago, it's nice to crawl back in once a day or a few times a day, it feels natural." Tory sees the ocean as his Creator, so to him it makes sense that he feels at home in the ocean, returning to it daily by surfing. When asked whether he has any surfing rituals, he notes "right as I get knee-deep in the water, I look in the ocean and say 'Thanks for letting me enjoy you right now', then dunk my head and go surf. A lot of people wait to get their hair wet…I do it right away." I immediately think of a Catholic dipping his or her fingers in the holy water and crossing his or herself when stepping into a church, recognizing the entrance into the House of God, a holy place. Dunking his head, Tory blesses himself with and recognizes the holiness of the Ocean. Saying a prayer, he shows his gratitude and love for it.

---

[10] Tom Blake- one of the world's most influential surfers. From Warshaw.

Similarly, Steve notes gratitude and respect for the ocean as the rules of surfing conduct which he considers key, describing "post-surf thanks to the ocean and respect for the environment in massive amounts" as that which one should practice. He also says that in return for what the ocean has given him, he feels a moral obligation to spread knowledge of surfing and the importance of respecting the ocean and the environment.

The ocean as an all-knowing and powerful entity is also not an uncommon theme in established forms of spirituality. Zen Buddhist surfer Jaimal Yogis sees surfing as an opportunity to learn how to attain the Buddhist goal of awakening, of becoming a Buddha. He writes

One of the historical Buddha's very first teachings…says 'the Earth expounds Dharma,'[11] meaning, I think, that the very world we live in describes how to awaken. And since most of the earth is ocean, I don't think it's going too far to say that, with the right attention and awareness, you can learn to be a Buddha by playing in the waves.

In other words, Buddha teaches that the earth contains all the wisdom necessary for enlightenment, for, by our definition, spirituality. It holds the potential for spiritual experiences. Since the majority of the earth is ocean, the way Jaimal sees it, in Buddha's terms the ocean contains some ultimate wisdom and truth. If one seeks this wisdom meticulously enough through spending time in the ocean, one has the potential to attain it. Indeed, like Jaimal, many a surfer connects with his or her own form of the divine through surfing- be it the ocean itself or another divinity.

---

[11] Dharma- Truth, Law, the doctrine and teaching of the Buddha, Buddhism. From *The Heart of Dogen's Shobogenzo*, translated by Waddell and Abe. (3)

8 THE SPIRITUAL EXPERIENCE

"When you're surfing, you're living. Everything else is just waiting." – Josh Mitchell, pro athlete, surfer

Evidently, it is no wonder surfers revere the ocean. Distinctly different environmentally and experientially from land life, the ocean provides an ideal environment for spiritual experiences to occur, and surfing the prime means through which one can live such experiences. Surfing if a prime example of an act sparking altered physical, mental and emotional states co-created with the ocean. This concept of a transformation of consciousness was not foreign to my informants, and the vast majority, twelve out of fourteen, reported experiencing an altered state while surfing, although they encountered difficulty when trying to describe such states, as they are ineffable. As we have established this type of ineffable transcendental experience as the cornerstone of spirituality, let us explore it in greater detail in this section.

Danger and Novelty

Surfers express feeling an indescribable feeling when in the water, saying there is "something happening" when they surf. Paradoxically, surfing feels completely novel, but simultaneously very natural, they say. As magazine editor Michael told me "surfing is a sanctuary where I feel a strong connection to something ultimately unknowable." According to surfer Steve Kotler, author of *West of Jesus: Surfing, Science and The Origins of Belief*, "There seems to be something in surfing that produces self-transcendent states more often than in other sports." When one considers the elements of "danger" and "novelty" of the surfing situation, one "begins to understand the potential for serious neurochemical reaction…the more we perceive the situation as unique, the greater our need for neurochemical response." In other words, the more dangerous, difficult and novel a situation seems to us, the more likely we are to enter into a physically altered state of consciousness, to have a literally extraordinary experience.

How does this correspond to surfing? Well, it is practically impossible to completely prepare for surfing. No wave is the same as the one before it. The shape, texture, height, length, weight, power, and speed of each wave, varies. Weather patterns are unpredictable- from one minute to the next swells can rise in feet and wave speed can quicken. The sun, tides, wind and the more immediate threat of waves and currents all factor into the equation of a surf session. Thus, surfing is an activity with consistently high risk and novelty factors, which means the likelihood for, as Steve says, "serious neurochemical reaction" while doing it, increases greatly.

"The Feeling"

Surfers use a plethora of language in attempt to describe this experience, yet most argue that no language does surfing justice: it is ineffable. Some surfers say this is the reason they are mistakenly stereotyped as brainless beach bums- they are often men of few words. To the general population they seem lacking intellectually. From the surfer's point of view, however, as one surfer put it, "Once you've seen God, what's there to talk about?" In other words, once one experiences surfing, nothing else matters as much as surfing. Nothing holds equal weight. Let us examine some surfers' attempts to describe their experience, and to support this claim.

Steve spoke about "The Feeling." He said that if one has not yet experienced "The Feeling," one cannot comprehend it. He thinks surfers have discovered a secret sacred path, and "whether it is a true spiritual experience or not, it is *real*." Steve previously suffered from Lyme disease and credits surfing to saving him. While sick he took up the sport and was transformed; he found himself "believing in surfing," he says. He compares these transcendental surfing experiences to Buddhist meditation because they not only require intense focus, but involve a loss of self or ego; namely, a transformation of consciousness, an experiential state which meditation often seeks to attain. Giving an example, he describes an experience he had while surfing in New Zealand, writing,

> *I paddled fast to my left, angled toward the next wave, stroked and stood, felt the board accelerate, and pumped once and into my bottom turn--- and then the world vanished. There was no self, no other. For an instant, I didn't know where I ended and the wave began.*

This kind of self-less experience often creates a feeling of either unifying with the all, the ocean, the divine- "For an instant, I didn't where I ended and the wave began," or, of nonexistence, nothingness – "There was no self, no other." Both experiences are gratifying for surfers: the former because, as I discussed earlier, connecting with the ocean, the power of nature, can be energizing, empowering, humbling and ego-boosting; the latter because if one experiences oneself as nothing, one escapes the pain, suffering and worries of life. One can lose oneself in the experience, and forget about work, school, and so on. Mitch agreed, telling me he compares it "honestly to a meditation." He said,

> *I'm not a religious person whatsoever but it's the one thing as close to religion as possible because you're so devoted to it. No one- unless they surf- knows the experience whatsoever. And everybody else wonders why you can put in 2-3 hours a day every day doing this thing, but no one else knows what it is until they try it.*

Again we see this theme of surfing as utterly novel, unique, incomparable to other experiences and incomprehensible to any non-surfer- of surfing as ineffable.

Bob's Malibu Magic

In an effort to convey the unique beauty of the surfing experience, my neighbor Bob told me a story about him surfing in 1971 at Malibu at age 16.

> *The big thing was surfing Malibu at night on a full moon because it was crowded during the day. Just bought a new surfboard, a Rick's red, white, and blue board. My best friend Jody picked me up from work, headed right for Malibu at 11, 11:30 PM. Went and surfed Third Point, it was a full moon and all phosphorous, with all the plankton. Every time we'd paddle it'd be this glow…probably the best wave I ever surfed at the time. We surfed from 11:30 till about 3, 4 AM. It was the most magical thing because every time you'd paddle it'd be all fluorescent and every time you'd catch a wave it'd be this glow…*

I'd like to note that Bob is a big burly guy who first seems rather aloof and reserved, but in reminiscing about surfing grows open, friendly and nostalgic. This isn't to say nostalgic in the melancholy sense of the term, but rather in a positive light. The underlying central role surfing plays in his life shown clearly. Though when asked he denied surfing as his source of spirituality, the tone of voice (heartfelt), spirited language ("magic," "glow") and graceful manner in which he related his surfing experience, told me otherwise. A statement he later made confirmed my inkling and contradicted his denial. He said, "There is a certain spirituality to surfing because I know when I'm being held underwater it becomes spiritual then." That is to say, when the ocean asserts its power, such as by holding one down underwater, one is forced to surrender to the ocean's will and recognize the reality of the situation, namely that one is powerless in the face of Nature. Consequently Bob's spiritual feeling here is likely one of humility similar to that of religious humility. One recognizes one's triviality in the face of a greater power.

Water

Surfers also cannot emphasize enough the importance of water in creating these experiences. Zen Buddhist surfer Jaimal explains how the more time he spends in the water, the more he feels like water himself. Surfing shapes you, becomes you. He says,

I've been surfing a lot lately, and there's something different about the saltwater life. One becomes floppy, like seaweed, while at the same time agile, like an eel. One becomes, I suppose, more like water itself.

He notes that one develops character traits out of surfing. The flexibility and agility he refers to here permeate his daily activities, his mindset. When he encounters difficulties in life he finds surfing has put things into perspective for him. After experiencing the ocean, the petty worries of land-life seem minute, and he is able to let them pass rather than dwell on them. On the other hand, when a situation calls for courage and decisiveness, he is more than prepared to fulfill those obligations. This is namely where the laid-back, go-with-the-flow vibe, as well as the confidence and tenacity of most surfers originates. As Tory concurs,

It's good to be in water, our bodies are primarily made up of water, and every day when I get in the water, it's like 'Wow…!' when water hits your body, there's something happening to some people, and it happens to me.

Again we see this theme of the ineffable experience, and again the clear difference between land- and sea-based perspectives, the novelty of the wavy ocean environment. Although not all surfers believe, as Tory does, that they originated in the ocean, all of the surfers I spoke with share the feeling he experiences when in water, agreeing that there is "something happening" when they surf. They describe something ineffable, transformative and captivating.

As we have seen, in surfing the event of a transformation of consciousness is not the exception, but the rule. The combination of the novelty, difficulty and risk of surfing, and the distinctive, powerful, variable environment in which it takes place, together create the reality of surfing as a practice in which spiritual experiences occur and the possibility of a spiritual process materializes. These experiences are spiritual because surfers experience them as self-transcendental. In having these transformative or even out-of-body experiences, many surfers discover for themselves answers to the questions "why am I here?" and "What is my purpose?" This does not mean surfing necessarily provides an ontological story for all of mankind, but it can provide a story of the self for each individual, a sort of personal ontology. In other words, it can provide one with a sense of what it means to live, the meaning of one's existence, on a personal scale. For many surfers, by helping them discover this for themselves, surfing becomes an endlessly fulfilling spiritual process. It becomes a form of spirituality.

9 THE FINALE

The main purpose of this project was to draw attention to the deeply embedded societal assumptions which oppose the secular and the sacred, and to question their validity by showing surfing as both a secular and sacred process. I wanted to show how this mentality acts as a barrier to our ability to recognize that secular activities like sport, art and other non-traditional forms of spirituality contain spiritual potential. Importantly, this is not to say that established forms of spirituality are invalid, nor that surfing is the right way or only way for one to be spiritual. It is only to show that surfing is one more way, one more option for a real spiritual experience and a possible path to enlightenment.

As I discovered, my literary research and interviews largely supported my thesis. I found that not only society, but even surfers are sometimes disillusioned by this paradoxical mentality. These are namely the surfers who are caught up in the superficial masculine brawn which often accompanies wave-riding. They view themselves as warriors conquering waves, proclaiming themselves as Gods and disavowing surfing as a spiritual activity- that is, until a giant wave crushes them and they surrender. There are surfers "who tell you they hate all the spiritual mumbo jumbo," says Aaron, but ten minutes later they're describing a wave they caught "and you think 'my, that sounds awfully similar to someone describing a baptism!' Deep down, even they know it [is spiritual]." Indeed, in my interviews, even the surfers with the most masculine, secular-based view of surfing used sacred language to describe their activity. Their language is my evidence.

This blatant hypocrisy shone throughout my research, and when I found it used by even the most spiritual of surfers, I realized that, to my dismay, even my beloved sport was riddled with hypocrisy. As Michael noted, "I'd argue there are only three things surfers need to survive: waves, boards and hypocrisy." He continued, "All I have to do is look inside myself and I'll see the same fundamentalism, fear and self-righteousness that turned me off to organized religion in the first place." Yet although surfing highlights hypocrisy it is not the source of it. The high presence of hypocrisy in surfing is due to its individualized nature and its basis on personal desire. Basically, surfing emphasizes our most basic and most selfish instinct: desire. Therefore this was neither a religious flaw, nor a surfer's flaw; it was a human flaw. We all constantly desire, and when our desires conflict with others' this often causes hypocritical behavior. But wherefrom was this desire fueling all human action emerging?

Our desire stems from the human condition. Essentially, we do not inherently know the meaning of our existence, and so have a fundamental desire to figure it out. Unable to rest with ambiguity, we continuously search for and making meaning out of our experiences, but rarely do we truly experience even momentary transcendence. Yet as my data confirmed, surfers experience transformative experiences often. This is because surfing is a phenomenologically unique experience, something novel, ineffable and transcendental. It leads surfers to engage in a process of searching and finding personal meaning through surfing. This process of seeking and finding meaning, when centered around a transformative experience, is what I call spirituality.

Consequently what began as a study of surfing as spiritual became a study of the human condition and human nature, through surfing. I found that what I had meant by "spiritual" referred to the alleviation of the human condition. I discovered that surfing was the perfect means for studying the human condition and the resulting human nature. The human condition, and our obvious aversion to it, is the reason we have fallen into the paradoxical, hypocritical mentality. Unable to make sense of information without dividing and categorizing, we sometimes place things in opposition when they do not necessitate opposition. Our fear of confusion has caused us to obsess with paradox- though we would be slow to admit it- and live hypocrisy, for the purpose of control and understanding. Yet, as we have demonstrated, this perceived understanding is sometimes faulty.

It is considerably difficult for us to embrace ambiguity- at least in the West. I realized that my whole project is based on a very particular ontology; a very western theory of the nature of being based on the notion that life is naturally ambiguous. This causes us pain because we naturally crave knowledge and control. Because we can never have universal control, in this constant pursuit we are paradoxically in constant denial, inevitably always ending up where we started, as confused and lost as ever. That which we seek forever eludes us. That is, unless through certain phenomenologically unique experiences we have what surfer Tory calls "flashes of brilliance." In other words, subliminal, enlightening moments which lead us to greater personal understanding; what I referred to in this paper as spiritual experiences.

At the end of this study, there is still a great deal left unanswered. The focus of my study did not necessarily change from surfing as spirituality to the human condition; rather, I began with a largely superficial idea of spirituality and as I delved deeper and deeper, realized the rabbit hole that is this subject. No matter the angle from which one assesses spirituality, the human condition, and the like, one finds a lack of conclusion in the field. Every "answer" provides a new question, and so forth. One must learn to embrace the process of inquiry itself.

In this paper, I think the any inconclusiveness is largely due to the fact that we are discussing *personal* religion. By James' definition, "the acts, feelings or experiences of a practitioner in light of his form of the divine. Therefore the meaningfulness of these experiences is relative to the individual. Further, any explanation of these experiences will always be, no matter how detailed, inadequate. This is because no one but the actor in the experience actually experiences the experience. Only the surfer truly knows and understands what he felt while on a wave, and his language will never do the experience justice. However this does not mean the field of religion or human existence is not worthy of study; on the contrary, its inconclusive nature proves there is only more to learn and experience.

There were many thinkers and schools of thought whose theories would have proven immensely helpful in my paper. For example, had I recognized earlier that my theoretical approach to surfing as a transformative experience was, indeed, a phenomenological approach, I would have made good use of Kierkegaard. I might even have discussed indigenous religions, American Pragmatism, and more of William James. Beauvoir would have proved useful on the human condition. As well, in the future I would like to compare Santa Teresa of Avila's western mysticism with more from Zen Buddhism and Keiji Nishitani from the Kyoto School. It would be interesting to explore whether the way west and east discuss this topic is really a conceptual difference, as I believe Nishitani would argue, or merely a linguistic one.

The most provocative questions I found myself with regarded vindication as to using "spirituality" as opposed to another term (such as meaning-making). Why use it? Why do we want to be able to call this spiritual? What background or mentality causes surfers to use this term to describe it? Also, why not profane the sacred instead of sacralizing the profane? Do we have a desire to posit an element in our life that is spiritual? Is this just a western mentality? I will not pretend to assess all of these questions here, but I will discuss what I have concluded in relation to them, having completed this study.

The reason I focused on spiritual experience as opposed to meaning-making, and surfing as opposed to another generally meaningful experience, is because this type of novel, transformative, phenomenological experience is, for most people, rare. It varies from one's average daily (and also meaningful) experiences. Moreover, it is namely that which we all desire.

We are all wishing for something to take our breath away. From my personal experience, the interviews I held and the literature I researched, I found that as a society, we generally think that without ever having these experiences, we will never be as happy or fulfilled as those who have had them, and especially not as happy as those who regularly experience them. This is why surfing, as a transformative, often life-changing experience, is, for our purposes, a spiritual one.

My experience, research and interviews have shown that when applying my definition of spirituality to surfing, surfing is spiritual. Therefore I have determined that the secular and the sacred are in fact not diametrically opposed. Any phenomenologically unique activity, traditionally sacred or not, can be spiritual if we experience and perceive it as such. Our mission in life is perhaps then to find our "surfing," the thing which lightens the burden of the human condition, bringing us closer to ourselves and our version of enlightenment.

I hope that this paper brings awareness to the sacred versus profane opposition so present in our society today, one which I think, once internalized, hinders us from having spiritual experiences in everyday life. I hope that this awareness may spark openness in you, the reader, both personally, to new experiences and new paths of enlightenment, as well as openness to others who consider nontraditional secular venues sacred. I hope that you will be able to view secular in a new light. Indeed, I also hope that you will have gained a newfound respect for these paths and the people who practice them, be the path surfing or some other practice. Like Steve, who credits surfing to saving him from Lyme disease, you might just experience something you didn't think possible. Got surf?

10 STILL HUNGRY?

Interview Questions

1. Tell me a little bit about yourself and your relation to surfing- years of involvement, short or longboard, why, anything relevant.
2. How did you become involved in surfing? What initially drew you to it?
3. What does surfing mean to you? Why is it so special? What purpose does it serve? (mental, physical, emotional..)
4. In what ways has surfing helped you grow as a person? Soul search? Character-building?
5. What kind of traits do you think are valued in surfing culture? Do you agree with/follow these? What are your own personal surfing principles?
6. Do you have any pre-/post-surf rituals? (i.e. yoga pre-surf, no sex-pre surf, pray before surfing)
7. Do you participate in any other sports? How do those experiences differ from your experience in the water? Does surfing serve a different purpose for you?
8. How does surfing affect how you act outside the water? Do your actions on land reflect what you've learned surfing? Or is it the opposite? (ex. I'm greedy in the water, but on land I'd lend you $100; or, Surfing teaches respect, for oneself and others.)
9. Would you consider surfing spiritual? To what extent? Does it have religious qualities or is in a full-on religion? Can it be all of these?
10. What kind of symbolic, spiritual, religious or ritualistic aspects do you see in surfing? (Anything-concrete and abstract).
11. What kind of unity or disunity is there between all surfers? Is there a basic connection?

BIBLIOGRAPHY

Allen, Michael A. *Tao of Surfing: Finding Depth at Low Tide*. IUniverse, Inc., 2007.

Bowker, John. *Oxford Concise Dictionary of World Religions*.

Brown, David, and Nick Ford. *Surfing and Social Theory: Experience, Embodiment and Narrative of the Dream Glide*. London: Routledge, 2005.

Cobb, Kelton. *The Blackwell Guide to Theology and Popular Culture*. Blackwell Guides to Theology. Blackwell Publishing, 2005.

Einstein, Albert. "Albert Einstein Quotes." http://thinkexist.com/quotation/true_religion_is_real_living-living_with_all_one/15625.html. (Accessed October 25, 2009)

Eliade, Mircea. *The Sacred & The Profane*. San Diego: Harcourt Brace Jovanovich, 1957.

"Enlighten," http://dictionary.reference.com/browse/enlighten (Accessed November 17, 2009)

Evans, Dylan. *An Introductory Dictionary of Lacanian Psychoanalysis*. Routledge, 1996.

Ferguson, Marylin. *The Aquarian Conspiracy: Personal and Social Transformation in Our Time*. Tarcher, 2009.

Fiona Bowie, *The Anthropology of Religion*. Cornwall: Blackwell

Publishing, 2006. (4)

Francis, Andrew, and Sylvie Shaw. *Deep Blue: Critical Reflections on Nature, Religion and Water*. London: Equinox, 2008.

Geertz, Clifford. *The Interpretation of Cultures: Selected Essays*. New York: Basic Books, 1973.

Giulianotti, Richard. *Sport: A Critical Sociology*. Cambridge: Polity Press, 2005.

Hebdige, Dick. *Subculture: The Meaning of Style*. London: Routledge, 1979

Hurston, Zora Neal. "Water Quotes." http://thinkexist.com/quotations/water/ (Accessed October 24, 2009)
James, William. *The Varieties of Religious Experience*. Kindle, 2007.

Kerby, Leslie. "From California to Costa Rica, *Pura Vida*." March 20, 2008, 1.

Kotler, Steven. *West of Jesus: Surfing, Science and the Origins of Belief*. New York: Bloomsbury USA, 2006.

Kreeft, Peter. *I Surf, Therefore I Am: A Philosophy of Surfing*. South Bend: St. Augustine's Press, 2008.

Krein, Kevin. "Sport, Nature and Worldmaking." *Journal of Sport, Ethics and Philosophy* 2, no. 3 (2008): 285-

"Secular." http://dictionary.reference.com/browse/secular. (Accessed November 17, 2009)

"Spiritual," http://dictionary.reference.com/browse/spiritual. (Accessed November 14, 2009)

"Spiritual," http://encarta.msn.com/encnet/features/dictionary/Dictionary

Results.aspx?lextype=3&sea rch=spiritual. (Accessed November 14, 2009)

Steele, Taylor. *The Drifter.* 2009

Taylor, Bron. "Surfing into Spirituality and a New, Aquatic Nature Religion." *Journal of the American Academy of Religion* 75, no. 4 (2007): 923-951

Turner, Victor Witter. *Blazing the Trail: Way Marks in the Exploration of Symbols.* Tucson: University of Arizona Press, 1992.

Turner, Victor Witter. *The Ritual Process: Structure and Anti-Structure.* Chicago: Aldine, 1969.

Walker, Matt. "Keeping the Faith." *Surfing,* July 2008

Warshaw, Matt. *The Encyclopedia of Surfing.* Orlando: Harcourt, 2005

"What is noetic?" http://www.noetic.org/about/what_is.cfm (Accessed March 5, 2010)

Yogis, Jaimal. *Saltwater Buddha: A Surfer's Quest to find Zen on the Sea.* Somerville: Wisdom Publications, 2009.

LESLIE KERBY

SNAPSHOTS

Ventura longboarder and surf instructor Lawrence Taylor Ugale gets shacked. Photo: David Pu'u

SURFING AND SPIRITUALITY

Previous: Ventura local Jordan Novander, Nicaragua. Self-Photographed

A big part of surfing is sharing it. Larry shares the wisdom. Below, Larry schooling us all in his "brown banana" suit. Photo: David Pu'u

LESLIE KERBY

Me, post-bodysurf, on a killer Christmas Day 2011. The waves were so rough that day my second swim fin tore straight in half on a wave.

SURFING AND SPIRITUALITY

In lieu of snow…

Larry Ugale, one with the wave. Photo: David Pu'u

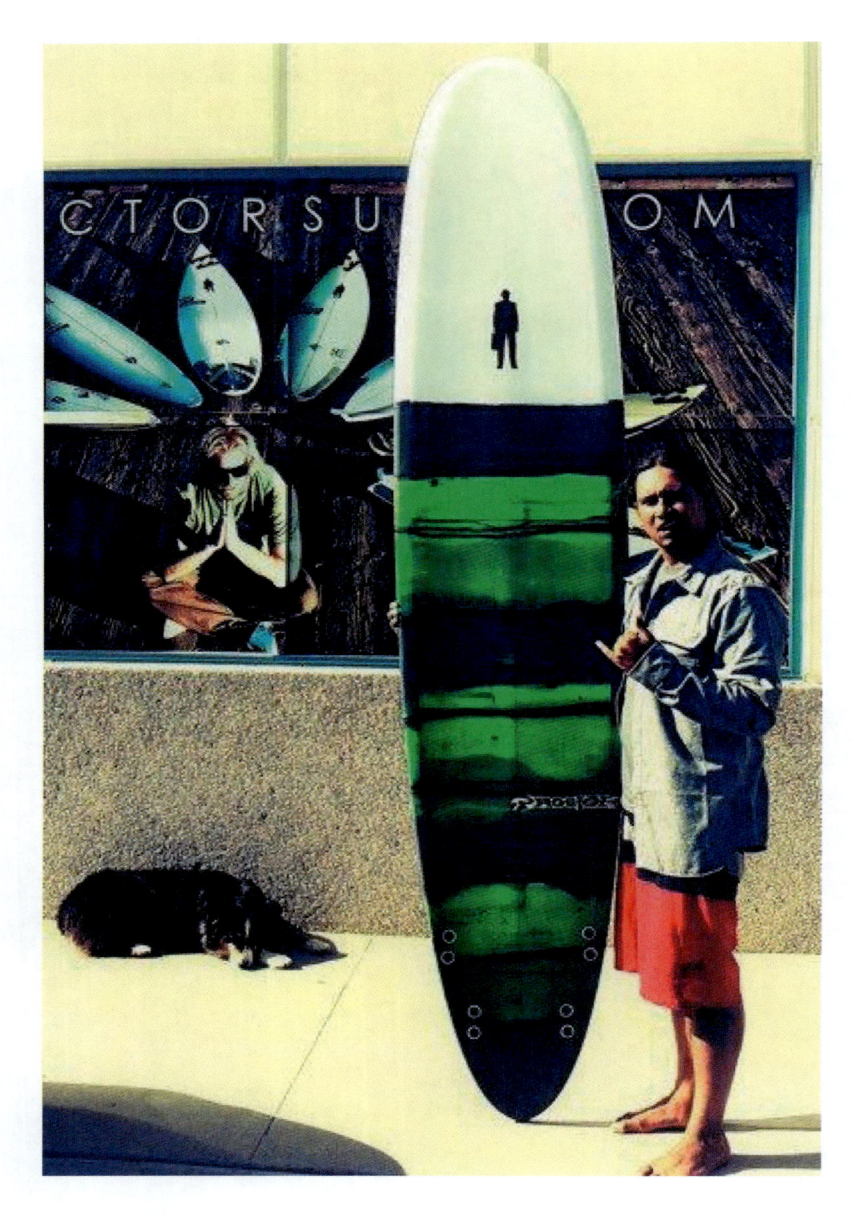

Larry again, this time uncharacteristically on land, with his faithful sidekick, Pu'alani. For surfers, boards = guns. Here: weapons of mass fun.

Timeless tube shot; Jordan Novander, Nicaragua 2012. Photo: GoPro/self

Previous: Sunset, Playa Hermosa, Costa Rica. Photo: Larry Ugale

Still surfing: interviewee Richard and best friend (later pro surfer) Mickey Muños, Malibu circa 1958. They both still surf daily.

SURFING AND SPIRITUALITY

"Into the Light" on a very good morning. Larry Ugale. Photo: David Pu'u

A perfect moment: Jaimal Yogis. Photo: Courtesy of Jaimal.

More Larry, more Pu'u- only the best.

Spread the word, share the stoke, and- most importantly- Enjoy the ride! Aloha, mahalo and blessings everyone. ~ LK

Surfing *and* Spirituality

LESLIE KERBY

Printed in Great Britain
by Amazon.co.uk, Ltd.,
Marston Gate.